The Magical World of Victoria the Friendly Ghost

Dean Rowell

Also By Dean Rowell:
Thomas and the Cat and Other Stories
Victoria the Friendly Ghost and Other Stories
The Further Adventures of Victoria the Friendly Ghost

Published by New Generation Publishing in 2022

First Edition

ISBN   978-1-80369-562-4

www.newgeneration-publishing.com

New Generation Publishing

CONTENTS

Chapter 1

A Day at the Palace

Isabel and Peter had arrived on a bright sunny morning in the summer to stay at Backworth Manor to visit Aunt Emma. This was a long time ago in Victorian times, when Queen Victoria was on the throne.

One day having lessons with their governess Mrs. Spence, the children heard a giggle behind the curtains. Mrs Spence had left the room and the children looked behind the curtains and there they saw a young girl, and Isabel and Peter gasped as they could see through her to the other side of the room. She wore a light blue dress and a cape of light green.

'Who are you?' asked Peter.

'Hi, my name is Victoria,' she said twirling around.

'Hi,' said Isabel. 'Are you a ghost?'

'Yes. Pleased to meet you,' said Victoria who curtseyed. 'Quick. Here comes Mrs. Spence! I'd better hide behind the curtain again. Haha.'

Victoria had been an orphan as a young girl in her life staying many years ago when Backworth Manor was an orphanage. She was among some children who suffered an illness and passed away, but now she was a ghost. Simpson was Aunt Emma's butler who stayed in his own cottage in the grounds and Mrs. Jones the cook lived near the Manor in her own cottage.

Victoria and the children became good friends. In the woods nearby, Victoria and the children ran and played games and enjoyed happy days. One day, Isabel and Peter were walking along a path in the woods with Victoria. The sun was shining and the birds were singing. Suddenly, the children saw a cottage they hadn't seen before. There was smoke coming from the cottage chimney. They knocked on the door and the door creaked open by itself very slowly. The children entered and Victoria glided forward with them.

Suddenly a hand was seen turning up a gas-light and a man appeared behind an armchair and he was dressed like a wizard wearing his hat and cloak, bearing a wand.

'Ah. Come in, come in,' said the wizard. 'I've been expecting you.'

'Yes. My name is Isabel and this is my brother Peter,' said Isabel. 'This is Victoria, who is a ghost and our dear friend.'

'Ho,' said the wizard, with a twinkle in his eye. 'I've seen you Victoria at Backworth Manor sometimes vanishing and re-appearing.'

Victoria curtseyed and twirled around smiling.

'Hi Wizard,' said Victoria. 'It smells like you're cooking something.'

'Yes,' said the wizard. 'This is my late lunch.'

A cat suddenly appeared.

'Ah. Wizard,' said Victoria. 'Your cat is saying hello to us.'

'You interest me, young people,' said the wizard. 'I have a special spell. Where would you like to visit most of all? '

'Haha,' said Isabel. 'Maybe go to Buckingham Palace and meet Queen Victoria.'

'Gosh, the Queen has the same name as you, Victoria,' said Peter.

Victoria laughed.

'All you need to do is step into the corner of my cottage, and I'll cast a spell, and it will take you to Buckingham Palace,' said the wizard.

The children asked Victoria for her guidance.

'Well, it's mid-morning, and I guess there's still time for an adventure before it's time to go back to Backworth Manor for an evening meal,' said Victoria.

'How will you bring us back?' said Victoria to the Wizard.

'Ah, in a moment, in the corner you'll see a blue mist,' said the Wizard. 'When you are ready to go the Palace, you will need to say these words, which I've written down for you.'

'Erm,' said Peter. 'Are you sure this is going to work?'

'When you are ready to come back,' said the wizard, 'just say these words…

Mist of blue, mist so true
Take us home, show the way
Mist of blue, friends are we,
Take us home, and there we'll be.'

'I'll write it down using a pencil in my pocket,' said Isabel.

'Just remember,' said the wizard. 'It may all be a dream, but you will be part of it.'

The children stepped into the blue mist when it appeared and then they found themselves in the garden of Buckingham Palace. The mist slowly faded around them as they stood in the garden of the Palace.

I wonder what year this is, or even a dream? thought Victoria.

Victoria kept to the bushes, in order to be out of sight since she was a ghost and did not wish to alarm anyone. Along with the children they arrived at a door, which the children opened and then went through another door, and they saw a lady asleep in an armchair, but she was dressed mostly in black.

Victoria hid behind the wardrobe, just in case the lady woke up and had a shock when she saw her. Isabel and Peter tiptoed past the burning fire in the grate to join Victoria. *Perhaps they could say hello to the lady and not stay a long time,* thought Peter.

'Who is the lady in the chair?' whispered Peter to Isabel.

'I don't know,' said Isabel.'We'd better not wake her up.'

Just then Peter knocked over a china tea-cup which fell off the side table and smashed. Suddenly, the lady in the armchair woke up with a start.

'Oh. I was asleep. I was dreaming,' said the lady. 'Who are you?'

Isabel and Peter knelt down, either side of the lady's armchair and smiled.

'My name is Isabel,' she said, 'and this is my brother Peter.' Peter stood up and bowed and sat down on the carpet again.

'That's a lovely spaniel that you have,' said Isabel.

'Who are you, ma'am?' asked Peter.

'Oh,' said the lady dressed in black leaning forward from the armchair, with a twinkle in her eye. 'Don't you recognize me?'

Isabel and Peter looked at each other.

'I am Queen Victoria.'

What! Oh my goodness, thought Victoria who was hiding behind the wardrobe. *Where has the Wizard sent us?*

Isabel and Peter cried out in amazement and stood up a distance away.

'I'm really sorry, my brother and I didn't recognize you,' said Isabel.

The Queen smiled, and seemed to change to a cheery mood.

'Don't worry, children. Here, come closer and take a seat either side of the settee.'

The spaniel barked and sprawled out at the feet of Isabel. Peter patted him.

The children laughed.

'Now Dash, be a good dog,' said the Queen. 'Ah. Isabel. You remind me so much of my daughter Princess Beatrice who lives with me here at the Palace. Peter, you remind me of one of my sons when he was younger. But you keep looking in the direction of my wardrobe? There is someone there isn't there? Children. Please invite your companion to come forward.'

Isabel and Peter looked at each other.

'Errm, Your Majesty. Our friend is behind you and her name is Victoria too.'

'How lovely!' said the Queen and she turned round in her chair. The gaslights were flickering and she couldn't quite see the figure, but she suddenly saw Victoria slowly glide towards her.

'Hello, Your Majesty. My name is Victoria too. I'm a ghost and I'm pleased to meet you,' as she curtseyed and smiled.

The Queen gasped and stood up.

'My word, my child. I can see right through you. Am I dreaming?' she said. 'Come further here by your friends where I can see you by the light of the fire.'

Victoria glided forward, her cape folding around her and she stood by Isabel and Peter and twirled around and laughed.

'I can sing and dance as well, Your Majesty,' said Victoria.

Isabel and Peter laughed as well and held hands with Victoria, although their hands passed through hers as she was a ghost.

The Queen laughed too.

'Ha ha. I am glad you are friends,' she said. 'I don't know, maybe I am dreaming, but I've not seen a ghost before, but I can't deny you've certainly brought laughter into my living room here.'

The Queen looked out of the window, and saw that it had started to rain. 'I lost my poor husband Albert many years ago, and that was sad,' said the Queen.

'I am so sorry to hear what happened,' said Isabel.

'Thank you, my child,' said the Queen. She thought for a moment. 'They tell me that there are starving children in the City of London. Do you know of these things? How can I help them? I see them from this window, huddled together in the street.'

'Have you some food in your Palace you can give to the children even tonight?' said Victoria. 'Our time here is very short. '

'Yes, I do,' said the Queen. 'But how do I get it to them, even at his evening hour?'

'Why don't we all sneak out with bags of food just now,' said Isabel.

The Queen thought of something. 'Young man. In that wardrobe, is a cloak and hood. If I can disguise myself, no-one will be able to recognize me. I have a plan.'

Peter fetched the cloak and hood for the Queen.

'I will call my butler and get him to bring a hamper of food. I'll tell him I'm expecting guests and he shall bring it shortly,' said the Queen. 'Victoria, you'd better hide behind the wardrobe, in case the butler sees you.'

Victoria nodded and hid by the wardrobe with the children.

'And try not to giggle,' said the Queen.

The manservant when summoned brought in a huge hamper full of delicious food including fruit, bread and cakes. When the manservant had gone, the Queen put on her cloak and put her hood over her head, in order that she couldn't be seen.

'Now then everyone,' said the Queen. 'Follow me.'

'We'll travel using my horse and trap to the street where I have seen the children who are in need of food. Victoria, you're a ghost so you can vanish and re-appear and then you can see the coast is clear before I take the horse and trap out of the Palace back gate!'

'Certainly, Your Majesty,' said Victoria.

'Now then, children,' said the Queen. 'Follow me. We'll climb down this drainpipe first and get into the stables this way. Oops. I'm not as fit as I used to be.'

Victoria had disappeared and re-appeared in the nearby street.

The Queen and the children went into the stables and led one of the horses out. As she readied the horse and trap to depart, her hood fell back, and one of the Palace footmen was passing and came to see what was happening.

The footman who was called Wilson recognising her said, 'Your Majesty, where are you going?'

'What do you mean, footman?' said the Queen, chuckling to herself. 'Have you never seen your Queen go out on an evening?'

The footman bowed apologetically.

'Come along children, hop on board. Footman Wilson, can you help us with this large hamper?'

The footman, wasn't sure what was happening, but helped to load the hamper on to the trap.

The Queen put her hood back over her head, and drove the horse and trap out into the street.

'Ho. This is fun,' she said. 'Hold on tight, children.'

Victoria appeared in the street behind a tree.

'This is where the starving children are, Your Majesty! Just round the corner by the park gates,' said Victoria calling out to the Queen.

The Queen nodded in acknowledgement

She stopped the horse and trap just around the corner at the park gates. Dash barked and Isabel and Peter helped to get the hamper down and open it.

As they did, a number of children dressed in rags came forward from the park near the Palace.

'Look,' said Victoria, out of sight, behind the horse and trap calling to Isabel and Peter. Why don't you put the food into separate bags using the paper lining from the hamper and give it to the children that way?'

'Good idea,' said Peter.

A few moments passed and Isabel and Peter shared out the bread and fruit and cake into small packages and gave them to the children. Some of them ate hungrily.

The Queen still wearing her hood stepped down from the horse and trap.

'Now then, children, don't forget to take some of the food home to your parents,' she said.

As she said this, the children came forward as they were really excited about the food. As they did so, the Queen's hood came down again and all the children could see it was Queen Victoria! The children suddenly became quiet after gasping! A boy took off his cap and the children bowed their heads. 'Gawd bless yer, yer Majesty. Thank you an all, for the luvverly grub!'

Victoria, decided that as she was a ghost she would hide behind some trees to ensure the children weren't frightened when she appeared. She saw the Queen step forward.

'Thank you, children,' said the Queen, trying not to shed a tear. Along with Isabel and Peter, she made sure everyone had something to eat.

One child, dressed in rags, came forward clutching her doll. 'Please miss, I never saw a Queen before. Cor Blimey. Pleased to meet ya.'

'Thank you,' said the Queen, as the children sat around her. 'Go home to your families, and take the rest of the food with you.'

'Three cheers for 'er Majesty,' said a boy who doffed his cap and the children left waving their goodbyes.

Victoria glided forward looking concerned.

'We need to be going home now,' she said to the Queen. 'Isabel and Peter's Aunt Emma will be waiting.'

'Let it be so,' said the Queen. 'Come along, Dash. Miss Isabel and Master Peter, please get back on board with the empty hamper.'

Victoria vanished and re-appeared back in the Queen's living room. They all climbed back on board with the hamper. Isabel held on to Dash as the Queen drove the horse and trap back to the Palace.

'My word. This was jolly fun,' she said and the children laughed.

When they arrived back through the gates, Wilson the footman came forward to take the horse and trap back into the stables.

'See that the horse is fed and watered, Wilson,' said the Queen. 'Come along children, let's go back into the living room and have something to eat by the warm fire.'

Isabel and Peter sat either side of the Queen and Victoria found a way of gliding forward so she was able to sit down on a chair with them.

'We have to summon the Blue Mist soon which will take us home,' said Victoria. 'It will appear at the end of the Palace garden.'

'Yes,' said the Queen. 'It would a good place for your Blue Mist behind the trees, where you won't be noticed. I thank you all for coming today. You have brought good cheer and song back to my living room after so many years. I saw the poor, starving children as well. I'll be speaking with my important friends and asking for some further help for them.'

'We'll have to be leaving soon, Your Majesty,' said Isabel sadly.

'I understand, children. You've told me about your Aunt Emma, and that she'll be waiting for you. Ah, children. I see the Blue Mist is in the garden of the Palace already,' said the Queen.

'Yes,' said Victoria. 'We need to be going now. Peter, have you written down the words we have to say to get back?'

'Oh my goodness,' gasped Peter, 'what have I done with it?'

'I have it, silly. It's in my pocket,' said Isabel. They both laughed.

'Quick,' said the Queen. 'Let's go into the garden now, so we're unnoticed.'

She walked with the children into the garden with Dash the dog barking beside her.

The Blue Mist appeared and together there was a great gust of wind.

'Victoria' said the Queen. 'Make sure you look after Isabel and Peter.

'I will, Your Majesty,' she answered and curtseyed.

'Miss Isabel and Master Peter,' said the Queen. 'This may be a dream for you which the Blue Mist has created and maybe this is a dream for me too, but I can meet with my ministers to see what more can be done to help the starving children. Thank you for reminding me of these things, children. It was nice to meet you.'

Isabel and Peter ran forward to the Queen to embrace her. Dash the dog jumped up and down as if to say he was happy dog.

'Ho,' said the Queen hugging the children 'What's this? Tears? Do not worry about anything. Everything will be fine. Give my regards to your Aunt Emma. Victoria, you too give me your hand too. I know my hand will pass through yours, but I shall remember you as well.'

'Thank you,' said Victoria.

Victoria glided forward and they embraced each other.

'Children, quickly run now into the Blue Mist. Your Aunt Emma is waiting for you. Victoria, look after your friends!'

'I will,' said Victoria.

'Bye, Your Majesty,' said Isabel and Peter, waving.

The three of them were within the Blue Mist and chanted:

'Mist of blue, mist so true
Take us home, show the way
Mist of blue, friends are we,
Take us home, and there we'll be.'

They vanished along with the Blue Mist and found themselves back in the Wizard's cottage.

As, they departed, the Queen had stood alone in the garden. 'Come along now, Dash. Time to go indoors for your favourite meal. Princess Beatrice will be here shortly.' Dash barked in approval.

Once in the living room Queen Victoria sat down in the armchair and wrote an entry in her diary. She then fell fast asleep with Dash, sleeping at her feet. Suddenly, she woke with a start when her daughter Princess Beatrice came in.

'Oh Mama!' said Beatrice, stoking the fire and putting the fireguard up against the fire and turning up the gaslight.

The Queen opened her eyes and Dash barked and woke up.

'I was asleep, Beatrice, and now I'm awake. Things I feel are going to be different now and it has been a long afternoon,' said the Queen.

Beatrice called the manservant to fetch fresh tea and scones and she sat down with the Queen by a roaring fire.

'Fetch me pen, ink and paper please, Beatrice. I want to write to an important friend to ask him to help the starving children in our city,' said the Queen. Princess Beatrice offered to write down what she wanted to say. The Queen thought to herself, *Victoria, Isabel and Peter, may it be a safe journey home for you.*

Victoria and the children meanwhile had arrived back at the Wizard's cottage and started their journey back to Backworth Manor in time for their evening meal.

'I'll vanish now and re-appear,' said Victoria after she had led the children through the dark woods.

'See you later,' she whispered and then vanished. The children went back to their bedroom.

'Children,' called Aunt Emma. 'It's time for your meal.'

'Goodness me,' said Peter walking down the great staircase of the Manor. 'Did we really meet Queen Victoria?'

'Maybe it was all a dream,' said Isabel.

Isabel and Peter later sat down at the table whilst Simpson served. Aunt Emma came in and sat down.

'Now then children, where did you go to today?' she said.

'Ha ha,' said Isabel. 'It was just an ordinary day really.'

'Yes, we were out in the woods today,' said Peter.

'That's nice,' said Aunt Emma. 'Simpson, you may serve the main course now.'

Isabel and Peter both giggled and looked up to the bannisters where they saw Victoria. Victoria winked at them and they winked back unnoticed by Aunt Emma.

Victoria laughed, twirled around and vanished. It had certainly been a lovely day!

Chapter 2

A Mystery at Backworth Manor

One afternoon, Isabel and Peter had finished their lessons with Mrs Spence, their governess.

'That's all today, children. Don't forget the poetry that you have to learn this evening,' said Mrs Spence.

'Oh no,' whispered Peter to Isabel. 'More poetry to learn.'

'Haha,' replied Isabel to Peter. 'We'll just have to help each other.'

As the children went back up to the staircase, they heard Aunt Emma opening and shutting the drawers in her bedroom.

'Oh dear,' said Aunt Emma. 'Where is my necklace? I can't find it.'

Isabel stepped into her bedroom. 'What has happened to your necklace, Aunt Emma, and what does it look like?'

'It's a necklace of pearls with a small sparkling bauble in the middle. It was a family gift. I could have sworn I put it in my top drawer here.'

Isabel and Peter later were sitting back in the living room by the fire eating a plate of biscuits. They left the plate of biscuits and went out to play in the grounds of the Manor.

They re-entered the living room and suddenly found that the biscuits on the plate were gone.

'Surely it can't be Twinkle the cat,' said Peter. 'I don't think she likes biscuits very much.'

'Oh no,' said Isabel. 'Could it be that there's a thief in Backworth Manor, and they're hiding somewhere?'

Simpson the butler just then had come in to stoke the fire and take away the plates.

'I know,' whispered Peter to Isabel. 'Let's call for Victoria.' The children went up to their bedroom.

'Victoria, Victoria,' they called.

'Here I am,' she said, appearing suddenly with her cloak waving around her as she swirled around.

'Victoria,' said Isabel. 'It looks as though there's a thief hiding in Backworth Manor. Aunt Emma's necklace is missing and, well, Peter and I were in the living room. Simpson brought in a plate of biscuits, and they were all gone when we left the room and went back in again.'

'Oh dear children,' said Victoria. 'It certainly is a mystery. I'll keep a look out for anything myself.'

Just at that moment, the children opened the bedroom door. At the foot of the stairs, they could hear Aunt Emma in the hallway calling Simpson to send for a messenger boy.

'Simpson,' she said. 'Send a message to Inspector Brown at Applethorpe Police Station. I want to report a theft that my necklace has been stolen.'

'Yes m'lady,' said Simpson.

Isabel and Peter were later in the living room playing a board game. Victoria appeared behind an armchair just as Simpson left, but then she saw the bookcase by the fire-place move slightly as though it had pushed open and pulled back again.

'Children,' said Victoria as she came forward. 'I think I know where the thief is hiding.'

She knelt by the chairs.

'The necklace was stolen, and so also were the biscuits. Surely whoever has stolen the necklace is still in this house,' whispered Victoria.

That night there was a storm, and rain beat against the windows of Backworth Manor and the wind howled. Isabel and Peter were fast asleep in their room. Aunt Emma had fallen asleep in the armchair. Everything was dark in the living room, as the gas-light had been turned down low and the fire embers glowed in the grate.

All was quiet as Victoria appeared and glided down the great staircase of the Manor unnoticed. Once in the living room, she thought she could hear a child crying. *Where is it coming from*? she thought.

Victoria wasn't sure, but it seemed to be coming from behind the bookcase. Then almost in an instant, the crying stopped. She could hear the crackling of the fire and Twinkle the cat jumped off Aunt Emma's lap as she lay asleep in the armchair and meowed and prowled around Victoria.

'Yes Twinkle, you heard the sound too?' she whispered.

Victoria vanished and re-appeared in the bedroom of Isabel and Peter and sat in the chair in the corner of the room, and watched over them as the rain beat against the window pane.

Suddenly, there was a peal of thunder and a bolt of lightning. Isabel woke up with a fright when she heard the thunder, holding on to her doll.

'Oh. What was that!, ' gasped Isabel still with her eyes half-closed. 'Victoria. Are you there? I'm scared.'

Victoria sat up from the chair. 'Don't worry, I'm here,' she said and knelt down by Isabel. 'It was a bad dream. Hush now.'

'Can you sing a lullaby song to us?' said Isabel. Peter had woken up but was still quite sleepy, and had heard the thunder and lightning.

Victoria sang a beautiful lullaby to the children and their eyes slowly closed and once again they fell into a deep sleep again.

Victoria thought about the sobbing that she had heard and how this may be connected to the missing necklace. She made sure the children were fast asleep, then turned around and vanished. Twinkle the cat then pushed their bedroom door open with her paw, jumped on to Peter's bed, curled up and fell asleep.

The next morning, the storm had gone, and it was a bright morning with plenty of sunshine. Inspector Brown had arrived at Backworth Manor along with a constable via horse and carriage to enquire further about the missing necklace.

Simpson showed them into the living room where Aunt Emma greeted the inspector.

'Thank you, Simpson,' said Inspector Brown.

'Now then,' asked Inspector Brown speaking to Aunt Emma, 'you mentioned that your necklace had been stolen.'

The constable opened his notebook to begin making notes.

'Yes,' said Aunt Emma who explained that she had kept the necklace in a box, and it was missing from her bedroom.

Isabel and Peter had entered the living room. Just then Inspector Brown, turned to the children and asked if they had seen any visitors to the house. Victoria was listening but out of sight to one side of the curtains. *Better keep out of sight, so I can't be seen*, she thought.

Inspector Brown also interviewed Simpson and Mrs Jones the cook.

'It's very sad, Inspector, I don't know where the necklace has gone. I feel so sorry for the mistress though,' said Mrs. Jones wiping her hands on her apron. 'Now, if you don't mind Inspector, I have two lovely pies cooking ready for the evening meal.'

'Thank you, Mrs. Jones. I shan't keep you. Well, Master Peter and Miss Isabel, I'll leave you and your Aunt Emma and I'm off now back to Applethorpe Police Station. If you find out any more about the missing necklace, just let me know,' said the inspector.

'Thank you, Inspector,' said Aunt Emma. 'Simpson will show you the way out.'

After he had gone, the living room was empty and Isabel and Peter sat around the chairs. Mrs. Jones was busy in the scullery.

Isabel leant forward in one of the chairs and whispered to Peter,

'I wonder if Victoria knows what happened to the necklace.'

'Yes,' said Peter, 'Let's call for Victoria.'

'Victoria, we're alone in the living room,' whispered Isabel.

Victoria appeared behind the armchairs where Isabel and Peter were sitting.

'Boo!' she said and the children laughed and turned around.

'Hi Victoria! Have you found out anything more about the missing necklace?' said Isabel.

'I'm not sure at the moment, but I wonder,' said Victoria. She moved toward the fireplace where Twinkle had curled up in front of the fire.

'Twinkle. Have you seen anything that could help us find a missing necklace?' she said.

The cat meowed several times to Victoria and prowled around the base of the bookcase and then jumped into the chair and blinked her eyes.

'Oh my goodness, children,' said Victoria.

'What is it?' said Isabel.

'I can understand what Twinkle is saying. She's seen the bookcase sliding back in this room. It must be by this method the thief found their way into the living room,' said Victoria.

'But who is the thief?' asked Peter.

'I'm not sure,' said Victoria. 'Just leave the biscuits here.'

She began whispering in case anyone could hear her.

'You'll need to be awake in the middle of the night. Just light a candle and I'll visit you,' said Victoria.

The children retired for the evening. During the night, it was a strong wind which howled which forced the twigs on the branch to brush against the window. The children woke up and Isabel lit a candle. Victoria suddenly appeared to them.

'Come with me, children,' she whispered.

Isabel and Peter put on their dressing gowns and slippers. Peter took an oil lamp with him and turned it down low.

'It's time to go down the staircase to the living room children, and I think I can find for you, where Aunt Emma's necklace has gone to,' said Victoria.

Victoria glided down the staircase and the children followed her.

'Gosh. It's a bit dark,' said Isabel.

'Sssh,' whispered Peter to Isabel. 'You're making too much noise.'

'Oh. Hold that oil lamp up a bit more can you, I can't see where I am going,' she replied.

'Let's all go in to the living room, children,' said Victoria.

Just as they went in, Twinkle arrived and purred and prowled around the bookcase by the fireplace. The rest of the food was missing from the plate, that the children had left.

Just then, the children heard the crackling of the fire but also a quiet sobbing. Victoria turned to the children.

'Yes,' whispered Victoria. 'There's somebody behind the bookcase which must be a secret wall of some kind.' The children remembered that they had once found a secret passage in the library of Backworth Manor.

'Ah,' let's see, if there's a secret button or a lever that we could press that would open the bookcase,' said Isabel.

'That gas-light bracket is a different colour to the others,' said Peter.

'Try pulling it down,' said Victoria.

Sure enough, as Isabel pulled the gas-light bracket down, there was a creaking sound and the bookcase slid back. Victoria and the children looked inside what was a dark room and gasped when they saw two children dressed in rags. A boy was hiding behind a wooden crate and a young girl was curled up in a blanket the other side of the crate.

'Gosh,' said Peter. 'What are you doing here?'

'Oh,' said the boy, as he saw Victoria gliding nearer. 'Who are you? Are you a ghost?'

'Don't be frightened,' said Victoria smiling.

'Was it you that I heard crying late at night?' asked Victoria.

''Yes,' said the boy. 'It's my sister. I was feeling very sad for her. She's not very well.'

With the bookcase slid back, Isabel and Peter could see it was a small room, lit only by a candle.

'I didn't mean to do it, but we were both so hungry, so I took the cake and biscuits that were left on the plate,' said the boy. 'But I think my sister is quite ill at the moment as she wouldn't eat anything.'

'Is that a necklace in your sister's hand that she's holding on to?' asked Isabel recognising it as the necklace that Aunt Emma described was missing. She was also worried that the young girl was curled up and did not look very well at all.

'Yes,' said the boy. 'I heard you talking about Aunt Emma. The necklace looked so lovely and sparkly and I saw it on the floor in one of the bedrooms. I thought it would cheer up my sister so I put it in my pocket and gave it to her. But she is so weak now and helpless. Please can you help us?'

'You'd better wake Aunt Emma now,' said Victoria to Isabel and Peter. 'Then we can help the children. I'll vanish now.'

The children woke Aunt Emma who came down and called for Mrs Jones and Simpson.

'Oh my goodness,' said Aunt Emma when she saw the children. She wrapped a blanket around the girl and lifted her gently to the settee. Isabel put a cushion under her head, so that the girl could rest.

'Simpson,' she said. 'Can I ask you to take the horse and carriage and fetch the local doctor from Applethorpe.'

'Yes, m'lady,' said Simpson who left the room to go to the stables.

Mrs. Jones had come into the living room with two bowls of hot broth for the boy and his sister. Victoria knelt behind an armchair.

'We heard noises and just guessed it was a secret passage, Aunt Emma,' said Isabel.

'Here is your necklace, miss,' said the boy to Aunt Emma. 'I'm sorry, my sister liked the sparkle and look of it and it cheered her up a little.'

Aunt Emma asked Peter to wrap the necklace in a napkin and then put it in the table drawer behind the sofa. Mrs Jones had put some more coal on the fire, and let it draw to warm the place up a little and then made broth for Peter and Isabel too.

'Now then children, drink your broth, it's delicious and good for you,' said Mrs Jones.

Aunt Emma lifted the head of the young girl who seemed very tired and weak, and with a sip of the teaspoon, the girl ate some of the broth.

'Isn't that better?' said Isabel, kneeling by the sofa, and the girl nodded.

Dr. Smithson had arrived from Applethorpe and gave medical attention to the children who had it seemed been in the secret room for several days.

Aunt Emma asked Simpson to prepare a room for the children, so that they could have a good night's sleep in a warm bed.

The doctor gave medical attention to the boy and girl.

'Aunt Emma,' said the doctor. 'The girl will need a lot of rest, and some food. She is slightly weaker than the boy. Thank goodness you found them in time Master Peter and Miss Isabel.'

Peter winked at Victoria behind the armchair and she winked back at Peter.

'Let me know how the children are in the morning,' said Dr. Smithson.

'I can pay you at the end of next week,' said Aunt Emma.

'No need for the payment, I was on a late call anyway,' he replied. 'Feel free to call me again, and I'll just put in on account. Mrs Jones, your chicken broth will work wonders I'm sure.'

Simpson took Dr. Smithson back to the Applethorpe surgery in the horse and carriage. Aunt Emma then made arrangements for the boy and girl to wash and be supplied with fresh night clothes to sleep and beds to sleep in, in the spare room.

Isabel and Peter came into the room with extra blankets for the children. Mrs Jones came in, and asked the children if they had sufficient broth, and they nodded. After Mrs. Jones had gone, Victoria re-appeared in the room but remained out of sight next to a wardrobe.

'Thank you for the broth. My name is John and my sister is called Hilda. I didn't mean to take the necklace,' said John to Aunt Emma. 'I thought it would be a nice gift for Hilda, as she had begun to feel quite ill.'

'How did you find it?' said Peter sitting on a chair by the corner of the room

'The necklace was on the floor in your Aunt Emma's bedroom,' replied John. 'We had run away from the orphanage a long a way away at Rosevale and we found refuge here at Backworth Manor. We heard that the Manor had secret passages where we could hide. Each night I would open the book-case and step out from the secret room where we hid. Hilda began to feel hungry and so we ate the biscuits and cake. Thank you for helping us, Isabel and Peter.'

'Thank you for what you have told me, about the necklace and now it is back,' said Aunt Emma. 'Sleep well, children.'

'He didn't mean to take it,' said Hilda weakly although feeling much better.

Isabel sat on the bedside chair.

'Don't worry, Hilda. It's time to rest,' said Isabel. 'Here is one of my dolls you can have.'

'Thank you,' said Hilda, beaming. 'Your doll is lovely. I'll call her Jemima.'

Aunt Emma smiled. 'It's all over now. Perhaps you didn't understand. Don't worry about the necklace. It's back now.'

After Aunt Emma had left, Victoria glided forward from the side of the wardrobe. Twinkle pushed open the door with her paw and jumped on to Hilda's bed as if to say hello and purred.

'This is Twinkle, our friendly cat,' said Peter.

'Hi Twinkle,' laughed Hilda and stroked her, feeling much better.

'Everything will be all right now, I'm sure,' said Victoria. 'John and Hilda, you need to get a good night's rest. Aunt Emma knows that the necklace wasn't stolen.'

John and Hilda mentioned how they had been unhappy at the orphanage at Rosevale, and thus sought refuge at Backworth Manor.

The next morning, Aunt Emma met with Inspector Brown and told him, that she had simply misplaced the necklace and that now it had been found. John and Hilda stayed at Backworth Manor for a little longer and Hilda became quite well again. In the glade in the grounds of the Manor, Victoria along with the children would dance around and laugh and giggle. Victoria would vanish and re-appear in another place just to tease them.

One day, John and Hilda were invited to another orphanage nearby which they liked very much and it was not far from Hindlebury Children's Hospital in Applethorpe. A horse and carriage arrived to take them to their new home. The children hugged each other and unnoticed Victoria appeared to them to say farewell.

'Thank you, Victoria, Isabel and Peter, for your all your help and kindness,' said John.

'We are friends always, and thank you for Jemima the doll,' said Hilda with a broad smile and feeling so much better.

'We are friends always,' said Victoria. They all waved goodbye to each other, and Victoria twirled around and vanished as the horse and carriage pulled away. As time went on, the children would have further adventures with John and Hilda and they became great friends.

-oOo-

Chapter 3

At the Court of King Henry

Victoria along with Isabel and Peter during one Saturday afternoon walked past a stream in the woods next to Backworth Manor and they came to a path that led to a bridge.

'Isn't that the path that leads to Pixie Cottage where the Tingleberry pixies live?' asked Isabel.

'Yes,' said Victoria.' We brought Aster their youngest son, some milk when he was ill so he could get well quickly'.

Victoria walked in front of Isabel and Peter, as the sun peeped through the trees of the forest and the butterflies were fluttering around them.

'Look,' said Peter. 'Let's go across the bridge and pop in and see the Tingleberrys.'

Victoria and the children walked to the cottage, and there they saw their pixie friends Timon and her brother Aster playing outside. Their gardener also doffed his cap and said, 'Hello'.

Timon and Aster invited Victoria and the children in for tea. The Wizard from his own cottage had also come to visit the Tingleberrys as well as he was passing.

After Mr and Mrs. Tingleberry had greeted them all and bid them welcome, they had some tea. Mr Tingleberry then had a nap by the fire with Hector the dog by his side whilst Mrs. Tingleberry was busy in the kitchen.

'Hi again, Mr. Wizard,' said Peter.

'Now then, Master Peter would you like to visit another place for a special trip?' said the Wizard.

'The Blue Mist again?' said Victoria.

'I've heard a lot from our governess Mrs. Spence about Prince Edward who became Edward VI,' said Isabel.

'It's a Saturday, children, so you mustn't be late back or Aunt Emma, will start to get worried about you,' said Victoria.

'Remember, the Blue Mist may take you to what is simply a dream and it may not be real at all,' said the Wizard.

Timon said she had some Pixie homework to do, and Aster wanted to help his mother with the washing up. Victoria, Isabel and Peter between themselves thought about where they could go.

'We could have a quick adventure I guess,' said Peter.

'Okay children, it's a quick visit and then home for tea,' said Victoria. 'We haven't had a special adventure for a while.'

The Wizard waved his wand and sparkles suddenly appeared everywhere. The Blue Mist slowly appeared in the corner of the cottage.

'Don't forget the card with the words to bring you back,' said the Wizard. 'Remember in our time, you will only be gone a few minutes.'

'I have the card here in my pocket from last time,' said Peter.

'Are we going to see Queen Victoria again?' said Isabel.

'Oh, somewhere else I'm sure,' said the Wizard.

Victoria, Isabel and Peter stepped into the Blue Mist which then carried them away.

'Oh wait,' said the Wizard, 'Oh dear. I haven't finished the spell yet. I wonder where they have gone? Ho.'

Once the Blue Mist began to fade around them, the children saw they were in another huge garden.

'Oh my goodness,' said Victoria. 'I remember this building from my childhood. We are at

Hampton Court Palace! But what year is it I wonder?'

'I remember. I mentioned the name of Prince Edward who became Edward VI,' gasped Isabel.

Just at that moment, a young man in Tudor costume wearing a sword, walked past some trees on a path in front of them. With her hand upon his arm, there was a young lady dressed in a flowing white robe, and she was adorned with jewels.

Victoria hid behind some trees, so that she couldn't be seen as the young man approached them.

'Hello,' said the young man to Isabel and Peter. 'How do you do. My name is Prince Edward. This is my dear sweetheart Lady Eleanor.' Eleanor curtseyed. Isabel and Peter stood with their mouths open in absolute disbelief.

'Oh my goodness,' said Peter, 'we are back in the Tudor times!'

'How do you do,' said Isabel who also curtseyed. 'I am Isabel and this is my brother Peter.'

Prince Edward laughed. 'Yes, indeed this is the time of the Tudors! But my word, young friends. How strangely you are dressed. You are visitors to Hampton Court?'

'We're certainly visitors,' laughed Isabel.

'Welcome to Hampton Court,' said Lady Eleanor.

Just at that moment Prince Edward noticed Victoria behind the trees.

'Oh. By all the saints. It is a spirit?' said the prince. 'Are you a friend of the children?'

Victoria decided to come forward and she curtseyed to Prince Edward and Lady Eleanor.

'My name is Victoria,' she said.

'I've never seen a ghost before,' said Princess Eleanor, 'but you and your friends are welcome at Hampton Court.'

They all began walking across the gardens behind Hampton Court surrounded by great fir trees.

'Ah yes, you are welcome here with your happy smiles, these are indeed troubling times.' Prince Edward walked forward for a moment, his cloak gently lifting in the breeze whilst he was deep in thought.

Victoria and the children walked with Princess Eleanor along the rosebushes.

'Yes,' said Princess Eleanor. 'Prince Edward's father is King Henry VIII who is uncertain about my friendship between his son who is heir to the throne, and myself.'

'Oh gracious me, are we really in the time of King Henry VIII?' gasped Peter.

'Perhaps we can all meet the King,' said Victoria. 'Then we can show our support for Prince Edward's happiness which means a lot to him.'

Prince Edward turned around to speak to the children.

'Ah, my friends, the King it seems has made up his mind, but the older he gets he is much comforted by his new wife, Catherine Parr.'

Isabel and Peter looked at each other and couldn't believe that they were here at Hampton Court Palace itself.

'Perhaps we can help the Prince and Princess Eleanor,' said Isabel.

'This may be a dream, but it certainly seems real,' said Peter. 'Remember in order to go back to our time, we have to call the Blue Mist.'

'In the meantime, let's see if we can help,' whispered Victoria to the children.

'Come my friends, you are my guests,' said Prince Edward. 'Let us go to the Great Hall of Hampton Court Palace.'

Prince Edward escorted by Princess Eleanor went into an entrance and thus into the Great Hall where tapestries hung round the walls.

Victoria quickly vanished and re-appeared but hid behind some chairs. *Surely that is King Henry himself who is sitting on the top-table? The Blue Mist has taken us back to the Tudor Times!* she thought.

It was indeed King Henry who sat in a big armchair at the top of the Great Hall where he was snoring whilst having a nap. There was a roaring fire, and a Great Dane was asleep by the fire. Prince Edward came in. Isabel and Peter started to tremble when they saw King Henry. They felt much more comfortable when they saw Victoria was with them in the Great Hall and she gave them a thumbs up.

'Is this really King Henry VIII?' whispered Isabel to Peter.

'Keep close to me,' said Peter. 'We'll just try and be as welcoming and polite as possible.'

Princess Eleanor stood with the children in the centre of the Great Hall, and they held hands. Victoria vanished and re-appeared behind a hanging tapestry out of sight.

Prince Edward had walked forward to the top table where the King was snoring.

'Greetings, my King,' said Edward clearing his throat.

The King woke up with a start.

'Oh my goodness,' he said. 'I must have dozed off. Ah. Greetings Edward, my son.'

The King noticed the children with Princess Eleanor, and saw that they were trembling slightly.

'Be not afraid. Young people come forth. Here sit by the fire, eat some food and be comfortable,' said the King.

Princess Eleanor smiled as she came forward with the children.

'Yes, Eleanor and Edward come forward also and be seated, you are my guests,' said the King.

Victoria thought it would be a good idea to be closer to the children. *I'd better show myself*, she thought. Victoria glided forward where King Henry could see her.

'By all the saints!' said the King as he sat back in his chair in amazement. 'Am I dreaming? Surely, it's a ghost.'

'Yes,' said Prince Edward to the King. 'Victoria is a ghost, and she is our friend, Oh King.'

'Ho-ho,' laughed the King heartily. 'Is she now.'

The King bade his guests welcome and sat down in his chair and sighed and looked out of the great window at the deer in the grounds of Hampton Court.

'Perhaps I am dreaming. No matter,' said the King. 'Victoria, I can see through you to the other side of the Hall. However did you arrive here? You will get home safely with your friends, won't you?'

'Yes,' said Victoria. 'I'll make certain they get home safely. It was the Blue Mist that brought us here.'

'A Blue Mist indeed? Tell me,' said the King after eating some chicken and throwing a bone to the Great Dane in front of the fire. 'In the land where you come from, am I known as a good King?'

Victoria wouldn't answer

'Haha,' laughed the King. 'No matter, no matter. I think I can guess.'

The Great Dane came forward and curled up in front of the top table and the King patted his head.

'Miss Isabel and Master Peter,' said the King, 'if you've finished your meal, warm yourself by the fire. Come forward too, Victoria.'

'Thanks, King Henry,' said Peter.

Princess Eleanor sat in the armchair by the fireplace and the children sat either side of her by the fire. The King's Great Dane decided to make its way over to the fire and sprawled out and barked and whined a little.

'What a lovely dog,' said Isabel.

'Yes,' said Victoria.' He is saying pleased to meet you. It's nice to make new friends'.

'Ha, ha,' roared the King. 'You're talking to the dog. What next Victoria? Will you be reading my mind?' You are a clever spirit indeed'.

Prince Edward walked over from the grand fireplace to the King.

'Yes Edward,' said the King. 'What is it?'

'Oh King. I would like Princess Eleanor to be my friend and companion,' replied Edward.

The King didn't answer and was deep in thought.

'Victoria,' chuckled the King. 'My minstrels will be here in the Great Hall soon. Do ghosts sing ballads, and perhaps I may thus be in a good mood to give Edward my consent?'

'Yes, please do sing, Victoria,' said Princess Eleanor.

The minstrels stood in the doorway of the Great Hall and strummed at the King's command. Victoria just out of their sight, sang a lovely ballad to their melody that she had learnt as a child when she was an orphan. In that moment, she thought of words of gentleness and good deeds.

There was a silence after she had finished, then Princess Eleanor, Prince Edward and the children applauded.

The King stood up and looked through the window again, deep in thought at the grounds of Hampton Court. 'Yes, thank you, Victoria. I don't understand this Blue Mist or even seeing a ghost for the first time, but that was indeed a wonderful song. You have brought the beauty of a sweet song into my Court.'

Prince Edward and Princess Eleanor came forward and the children applauded. The King stood looking at the fire in the hearth.

Prince Edward felt this was the right moment to ask his question again. 'My King. Do I have your blessing on my friendship with Princess Eleanor at Court?'

Victoria glided forward and looked at the King, putting her hands on her hips.

'Well, Your Majesty?' she said with a smile.

The King for a moment frowned, but almost in an instant roared with laughter.

'Ha, ha,' he roared. 'I am listening to a ghost. Ho, ho and why not. You are brave enough to stand up to a King!'

King Henry stood up beaming, 'Prince Edward and Princess Eleanor. You indeed have my blessing as friends and companions. The King is indeed pleased for you to be happy and attend the court.'

'Thank you, Your Majesty,' said Prince Edward bowing and holding Princess Eleanor's hand as she curtseyed.

Isabel and Peter came forward to hug Edward and Eleanor.

'Yay,' said Isabel. 'Happy times ahead!'

Isabel, Peter and Victoria then danced around in a circle together by the fire. Just then a footman came in and accidentally dropped a plate which smashed. The footman who was called Thomas then feared the wrath of the King and trembled.

The King stood up from his chair abruptly as though in a rage. The King though caught the eye of Victoria as she wagged her finger at him and whispered, 'Now King Henry, kind words!'

There was a pause. 'Ha ha,' roared the King. 'No matter, Thomas! Just send for the maid to clear up the mess.' The King reached inside his doublet. 'Here, Thomas. Here is a coin for your troubles, and may you look after your family well.'

'Thank you, thank you,' said the footman and picked up some of the broken plates and disappeared as quickly as possible.

'Now then Victoria! Did I do well?' said the King with his hands on his hips.

'You did well, King Henry, you did well!' said Victoria. Isabel and Peter danced around with her once again, holding hands with Princess Edward and Princess Eleanor.

The King roared with laughter. 'Come on, minstrels! Don't just sit there. Ha-ha. Play something!'

Prince Edward and Princess Eleanor then taught Isabel, Peter and Victoria a Tudor dance. There was much laughter and the children had some lovely food to eat. Later, King Henry let the minstrels return to their duties. Just then, the King gazed out of the Court windows and he saw the Blue Mist appearing outside in the grounds of Hampton Court Palace.

'Victoria,' said the King. 'You said you and the children came from the future. Maybe this is all a dream after all, and I don't understand it, but the Blue Mist you described is just beyond my fir trees by the lake beyond Hampton Court.'

'Will you be travelling back to your own land now?' said Prince Edward.

'Yes,' said Victoria. 'Come along, children, it's time to go home now. Quickly, children. The Blue Mist is here.'

Isabel and Victoria curtseyed before the King and Peter bowed.

'May it be a safe journey back to your land,' said the King. 'You have brought music and laughter back to my Court and for that I am grateful.'

'Yes,' said Prince Edward. 'You are welcome back to Hampton Court as our guests.'

The children, along with Victoria, ran down to the Mist in the great garden. Princess Edward and Princess Eleanor and the King came into the garden and stood back from the Blue Mist amongst the fir trees.

'Goodbye, children,' said Princess Eleanor. Just then Isabel and Peter ran forward to hug the Princess.

'Haha. Dear children, you are very kind,' said the Princess. 'Hurry now to back to your own land. Your Aunt Emma will be waiting for you. Victoria, look after yourself. I'll embrace you even though you are a ghost.'

Victoria and the Princess held each other.

The children and Victoria stepped into the Blue Mist.

'Goodbye, King Henry!' shouted Peter.

'Farewell to you, my boy. I shan't forget the joy of this fine day. Farewell back to your own time and look after your Aunt Emma.'

Victoria and the children chanted the words from the card that Isabel had kept in her pocket:

'Mist of blue, mist so true

Take us home, show the way

Mist of blue, friends are we,

Take us home, and there we'll be.'

The Blue Mist took Victoria and the children back to the Wizard at Pixie Cottage.

Following the departure of the Blue Mist, King Henry walked back into the Great Hall with Princess Eleanor and Prince Edward.

'May happiness be your portion, Edward and Eleanor,' said the King. 'Now I wish to sleep in my chair. My son, will you please ask Catherine my wife to come to the Great Hall.'

The King slept a little whilst his wife Catherine came to his side and the Prince and Princess took a walk in the Courtyard. The sun shone and the deer could be seen in the distance.

'Will Victoria and the children visit us again here at Hampton Court?' asked Eleanor.

'I'm sure they will. We will remember them and they are our friends,' said Prince Edward.

They returned into the Great Hall whilst King Henry slept in the chair, and the minstrels came forward and played again.

When Victoria, Isabel and Peter arrived back at Pixie Cottage, they stepped out of the Blue Mist.

'You were only gone a few minutes,' said Mrs. Tingleberry wiping her hands on her apron. 'There's still time for you to get home for your tea.'

'Where have you been?' said Timon playing her flute.

'Ha ha, it's long story,' replied Victoria.

The children went back through the woods with Victoria who vanished just outside the entrance to the woods. Aunt Emma greeted the children outside Backworth Manor.

'Out playing again,' she said.

They entered the Manor and washed their face and hands and came down to the dining room. Victoria re-appeared and hid behind the bannisters.

'Now then, children. Mrs. Jones has prepared our evening meal. Where have you been today?' asked Aunt Emma.

'Oh, we've been to see the King!' replied Peter half-joking.

'Ha ha, that's lovely,' replied Aunt Emma. 'We are ready to serve now, Simpson.'

'Yes, m'lady,' replied Simpson.

The children looked up at Victoria behind the bannisters who waved, smiled and disappeared.

-oOo-

Chapter 4

The Haunted Windmill

Mr and Mrs Allbright lived at Greenthorpe nearby to Applethorpe village and one day came to visit Backworth Manor. Isabel and Peter were being taught by Mrs. Spence, their governess.

'Who is that who has come to stop for tea and say hello to Aunt Emma?' whispered Isabel to Peter in the classroom.

'I'm not sure,' said Peter. 'But they live behind the woodland in Greenthorpe in a windmill.'

Mrs. Spence held her chalk in her hand at the blackboard and turned around after hearing the children whispering.

'Now then, children,' said Mrs. Spence. 'Pay attention. You'll have some homework to do this evening.'

'Oh no,' whispered Peter. 'More poetry to remember.'

'Haha,' replied Isabel. 'Perhaps Victoria can help us to learn it!'

At the end of the lesson, the children put away their chalks and pencils and wandered into the lounge by the foot of the great staircase where Simpson was serving tea to Mr. and Mrs. Allbright.

'Do you require anything to eat, Master Peter?' said Simpson.

'No thank you, Simpson,' replied Peter. The children sat on the settee wondering who the visitors were.

Mrs Allbright was in conversation with Aunt Emma, whilst she sat by the fire

'You know we live in a windmill behind the woodland in Greenthorpe,' said Mrs. Allbright looking agitated. 'Dearest Aunt Emma, in the middle of the night, we can often hear what sounds like a child crying, and then the bark of a dog. Mr Allbright one night lit a candle and we came downstairs, and we found that some of the chairs had been moved or knocked over. This has happened a few times recently.'

'Perhaps, this could be due to the wind blowing through the trees? Greenthorpe Windmill does seem to be up on a height?' said Aunt Emma. Just then Twinkle the cat walked in, meowed and curled up in front of the fire. At this time, Victoria appeared and hid behind the bannisters at the top of the stairs.

Mrs Spence had joined them for tea after the children's lesson.

'Will that be all for today, ma'am?' said Mrs Spence to Aunt Emma.

'Yes, thank you, Mrs. Spence,' replied Aunt Emma. 'I'll arrange for a pony and trap to pick you up tomorrow.'

Simpson cleared away the dinner plates.

'We'll take tea in the living room,' said Aunt Emma. 'Can you stoke the fire a little and turn up the gas lamps?'

'Yes, m'lady,' replied Simpson.

Mrs Jones appeared at the doorway wiping her hands in her apron.

'How was the meal this evening, m'lady,' asked Mrs Jones.

'Yes, the dinner was fine, Mrs. Jones,' said Aunt Emma.

Isabel and Peter slipped back up to their bedroom followed by Twinkle. Victoria disappeared from the bannisters and re-appeared in the bedroom with the children. Isabel and Peter asked Victoria if she heard what Mrs Allbright was saying, and what she thought about the sounds of someone crying and furniture being moved around?

'So they heard the sound of a boy crying, along with a dog barking?' asked Victoria. 'I had heard tales of the Windmill at Greenthorpe being haunted, but it seems at the moment that the windmill has a resident ghost?'

'Gosh,' said Isabel clutching her doll. 'Just think, Victoria! Another ghost! Perhaps you have a new friend in the area?'

'Ha ha,' said Victoria. 'I wonder who it can be? Hmm. In fact, I think I can guess who it can be.'

Twinkle purred as if in agreement.

'Perhaps we can all go up ourselves to Greenthorpe Windmill on Saturday and find out a little more about this haunting? It would be like solving a mystery!' said Peter.

'I know,' said Isabel excitedly. 'Let's go and see the Wizard in his cottage first, and then he can help us with some ideas?'

'Ho,' said Victoria. 'If it's a haunting I think I know who it is! Well, Twinkle, shall we go and see the Wizard in his cottage by the Manor?'

The cat purred and meowed.

'Yes, Twinkle,' replied Victoria. 'Okay, we'll visit the Greenthorpe Windmill to look around first and then we'll go and see the Wizard.'

'Yes,' said Isabel. 'We can call on the Allbrights and ask if we can visit their stables to look at their horses.'

'Oh well,' said Victoria. 'We'll all meet tomorrow evening to go up to Greenthorpe Windmill, but for the rest of the evening children…'

Isabel and Peter knew what was coming.

'You need to make certain you learn your poems this evening, that Mrs. Spence set you,' said Victoria teasing them.

'Oh no,' said Isabel and Peter. They laughed and took their poetry books out for their homework.

'But Victoria can we have a song tonight please?' said Isabel.

'Yes, of course,' replied Victoria. 'But Aunt Emma is coming, so I'd better disappear.'

Victoria vanished and the children began to learn their poetry whilst Aunt Emma came in to see if they were all right.

Later at nightfall, Victoria re-appeared to the children as they sat up in bed as the candle on the bedside table burned low. She sang them a song and slowly Isabel and Peter fell asleep whilst the rain beat against the window. *I think they're asleep now*, she thought. Victoria blew out the candle and disappeared.

The next day the sun shone for most of the day and Victoria along with the children made the journey through the wooded path to Greenthorpe Windmill and called at the home of Mr. and Mrs. Allbright.

Peter knocked on the front door of the windmill which was answered by Mrs. Allbright.

'Hi Mrs. Allbright,' said Isabel when the door was opened. 'We were just passing. I was wondering if we could have a look at your horses in your stable. They look so wonderful.'

'Hi Isabel and Peter,' said Mrs. Allbright. 'I've recently visited your Aunt Emma. Look, why don't you both stay for tea as you have come a long way from Applethorpe. Then you can say hello to the horses if you like.'

The children had some tea, thanked Mrs. Allbright and then went into the stables. There, out of sight, Victoria appeared to them.

'Let's wait until nightfall,' said Victoria. 'Then we can find out a little more about this mystery.'

Just then, two of the horses in the stable neighed and whinnied. Victoria seemed to understand what they were saying.

'Ah. One of the horses is saying that he's also heard the sounds of a boy laughing and a dog barking,' said Victoria.

'Gosh,' said Isabel. 'It's a mystery, isn't it?'

It was starting to get dark and the children were glad that Victoria was with them. At nightfall, some squirrels from the woods came and also spoke to Victoria.

Isabel and Peter came closer to Victoria.

'What are the squirrels saying Victoria?' asked Isabel in a whisper.

The squirrels at that moment sat on the stable fence making their sounds to each other.

'Children,' whispered Victoria. 'It is as I suspected. There's a ghost boy in the windmill with his ghost dog and they are somewhere around here now.'

'You mean he is a ghost like you?!' whispered Peter.

'Ha ha, yes,' replied Victoria gliding around with her cloak flowing around her. 'We need to find out where he is, and have a chat.'

'Perhaps, the squirrels can show us where this "ghost boy" is?' asked Isabel.

'Yes,' said Victoria. 'Squirrels. Can you show us where the ghost boy is?'

Isabel and Peter wondered what would happen next. Sure enough, the squirrels led Victoria and the children to a barn next to the stables. They went inside and saw to their amazement, the pale figure of a young boy and his collie dog, and they could almost see through their ghostly outline. The dog barked when he saw the children, and the boy and the dog quickly darted away to hide behind some boxes.

'Hi there,' said Victoria stepping forward. 'We know you are here, and we've come to help.'

The boy came forward slowly, but raised his head and smiled. Sure enough, he was very pale, and the children could see through him. He was dressed in a similar way to Peter.

'Hi there, my name is Victoria. These are my friends, Isabel and Peter,' said Victoria.

'Hello Victoria,' said the ghost boy. 'My name is Jack. I can see you are a ghost just as I am.'

When the children came forward, Jack stepped back into the shadows.

'Don't worry, Jack,' said Victoria. 'My friends, Isabel and Peter are used to seeing me.'

'Ha,ha,' said Jack, gliding forward. 'Thank you for coming to see me, Victoria. I remember you from the orphanage many years ago, but I wasn't sure at first. My dog is called Dexter.'

'Hi Dexter,' said Peter. Dexter barked as if to say hello.

'The Allbrights who live at the Windmill here, wondered what all the noises were?' said Isabel.

Jack suddenly moved to a corner of the barn and sat down and sobbed. Dexter sat down beside him and whimpered. Victoria came near to him along with the children.

'Gosh,' said Victoria. 'What is the matter? Perhaps we can help, Jack?'

'Sorry to see you upset, Jack,' said Peter.

Jack brightened up a little. Even though he was a ghost he found he was able to sit down on an old chair in the corner of the barn. Dexter stood on his hind legs and barked to cheer him up.

'Sorry, I was a little upset, but I remember as a boy, when I wasn't a ghost, the Allbrights reminded me of my parents, and I could see they were very kind.'

'Your parents before you became an orphan at Backworth Manor?' asked Victoria.

'Yes, that's right,' replied Jack. 'I would do anything to be a boy again, rather than a ghost. Then I could maybe ask Mr. and Mrs. Allbright to look after me?'

Victoria thought for a moment.

'I know a Wizard who lives in a cottage in the woods beside Backworth Manor where the children live', said Victoria.

'Gosh,' said Jack. 'Could your Wizard friend cast a spell and make me a boy again?'

'We'll see,' said Victoria.

The children spoke with Jack and they knew they had made a new friend. Victoria said she had a plan.

'I could appear to Mrs Allbright and tell her that it's a boy that's making the noises in the windmill. I won't say he's a ghost though,' said Victoria.

'Perhaps the Wizard can use one of his spells to make Jack into a boy again, just like me,' said Peter.

'I'll need to see Mrs. Allbright first,' said Victoria thinking to herself. 'Okay Jack, we'll meet you later.'

'Can you really help me and my ghost dog Dexter?' said Jack just as Dexter barked.

'Of course, we can try,' said Isabel.

Dexter barked again.

'He's saying he is pleased to see us,' said Victoria.

'Ha ha,' said Jack. 'You are a ghost that can speak to dogs and understand too what they are saying.'

The children said goodbye to Jack as it was evening and Aunt Emma would be worried about them. Peter, Isabel, Jack and Victoria hugged each other. Isabel put her arms around Dexter the dog. Although he was a ghost dog and she couldn't touch him, he seemed to know what was happening and barked and leaped around.

Jack said he was happy to be a boy again and wanted the Allbrights to look after him. Victoria said she would see the Wizard to see if he could help. They all danced around together and the children left Greenthorpe to go back to Backworth Manor as it was late.

-oOo-

Chapter 5

Victoria and the Wizard

Victoria had contacted the Wizard so that they would meet at Pixie Cottage in the woods along with Isabel and Peter. There they met together. Mrs Tingleberry was making tea and Mr. Tingleberry was snoozing by the fire, The Wizard walked through the door-way and knocked his tall hat off.

'Oh dear,' he chuckled. 'I forgot the cottage was a little small.'

Isabel, Peter, Timon and Aster giggled. Victoria explained to the wizard, that they had met the ghost boy Jack and his ghost dog Dexter at Greenthorpe Windmill and that Jack very much wanted to become a boy again.

'Well Wizard,' said Victoria. 'Can you help Jack? I think he would prefer to be an ordinary boy like Peter rather than a ghost.'

'Perhaps I can help him,' said the Wizard stroking his beard, thinking about the spells that he had in his book. 'Does he really want me to do this for him.'

'Yes. We've met Jack and discussed this,' said Peter. 'He would also like the Allbrights to take care of him. They think the windmill is haunted, but it's really just Jack and his dog.'

'Very well,' said the Wizard. 'If you tell Jack to come and visit me.'

'I am going to speak to Mrs. Allbright first,' said Victoria twirling around. 'I'll tell her that it's a boy called Jack with his dog who is making the sounds in the Windmill. I'll mention that he is looking for a home and would she prepared to look after Jack and perhaps foster him.'

'How are you going to do it,' asked Timon playing with her toys as she sat by the fire. 'Mrs. Allbright will find out that you are a ghost.'

'Somehow I'll need to find a way of speaking to Mrs. Allbright alone in the windmill,' replied Victoria.

Mrs Tingleberry came in with a tray ready to set the table. 'Timon and Aster, you had better wash your face and hands, as your tea will soon be ready,' said Mrs. Tingleberry.

'Can Jack really become a boy again like me, and then Mrs. Allbright can look after him,' said Peter.

'We'll see,' said Victoria.

Isabel and Peter left to go back to Backworth Manor and Victoria vanished after guiding the children back through the woods to the Manor.

The children the next morning had their lesson with Mrs. Spence and they wondered what Victoria would say to Mrs. Allbright at Greenthorpe Windmill and they found it very hard to concentrate.

'Peter,' said Mrs. Spence holding the piece of chalk in her hand. 'What is 2 x 2 + 4?'

'Oh. Sorry, Miss, I wasn't paying attention,' he replied.

'Gosh. You really must concentrate in future. Anyone would think you had seen a ghost.'

The children giggled but said nothing. *If only if you knew* thought Isabel.

'You both have generally done well though,' said Mrs Spence. 'Here is your homework for this evening, children.'

Victoria later that night appeared to Mrs Allbright at Greenthorpe Windmill. She was asleep by the fire, and Victoria was in a corner of the room just keeping to the shadows. Just at the moment, there was a gust of wind and the branch of a tree scraped its twigs across one of windows of the windmill. Suddenly, Mrs. Allbright woke up with a start.

'Oh my, what was that noise? I must have been dreaming,' she gasped. Just at that moment she saw Victoria in the corner of the room, lit up by the light of the fire.

'Oh my goodness! It's a ghost!' she shrieked and dropped a cup that she was holding so that it smashed on the floor.

'Don't be afraid,' said Victoria, gliding forward. 'I am a ghost and my name is Victoria, I came here to ask for your help.'

'I-I'm not sure what I am seeing,' replied Mrs Allbright and began to pick up the pieces of the broken cup. 'Let me stoke the fire a little. There now.'

Victoria smiled and sat by the fire with Mrs Allbright who felt a little more relaxed.

'How can I offer this help you are looking for, Victoria?' she said.

'The barking of the dog and sobbing at night-time around your Windmill. That was my friend Jack,' replied Victoria. *I'd better not mention that Jack was a ghost,* she thought.

'He really needs a home Mrs Allbright. Could you offer that home and look after him?' said

Victoria. 'Erm, Jack also has a dog called Dexter.'

'Oh my goodness,' said Mrs. Allbright holding her hands. 'This all seems like a dream, but I would like to help. I would need to discuss it with Mr. Allbright.'

'You mustn't tell him I'm a ghost,' said Victoria. 'I can count on you?'

'You can count on me, Victoria. I promise,' said Mrs Allbright, smiling. She was filled with joy that she had an opportunity to look after a young person and foster or even adopt a boy as her own child. Mrs Allbright said again that she would see her husband later to discuss it

'It's been a delight to speak to you, Victoria,' said Mrs. Allbright.

'Happiness to you and thank you,' said Victoria, and she vanished.

When Mr. Allbright arrived home later, Mrs Allbright spoke with him.

'Look, we live in a windmill here in Greenthorpe, but we are alone, John. I was thinking if you wanted to adopt a young boy so we could look after him. It's something we have spoken about before.'

Mr. Allbright put his pitchfork and tools down that he was carrying.

'Yes, it's something that I've been thinking about too,' he said. 'Of course we can look after the boy, if you are okay with this.'

'Great,' replied Mrs. Albright. 'The boy will be coming to see us soon and he will be with his dog called Dexter.'

'Well, I'm blowed,' said Mr Allbright putting away the garden tools. 'How did you know all these things, Martha?'

Mrs. Allbright remembered her promise not to tell anyone about Victoria since she was a ghost, and perhaps her story wouldn't be believed.

'Let's just say I guessed it would happen,' she said.

Mr. Allbright just shrugged his shoulders and led one of their horses into the nearby stable.

Later that day, Victoria appeared to Jack and his dog Dexter in the barn by the stables.

'You can come with me and the children to the Wizard's cottage, Jack,' said Victoria.

Jack and his dog Dexter disappeared along with Victoria and re-appeared at the Wizard's cottage. The Wizard introduced himself to Jack.

'Oh my goodness,' said the Wizard. 'Yes, I can see that you are a ghost. Well now Jack, do you want to be a boy again?'

Victoria smiled as Jack spoke.

'Yes, I would like to become like an ordinary boy again, and for my dog Dexter to be real as well,' said Jack.

'Ah,' said the Wizard stroking his long beard. 'Let's see what we can do as a spell.'

Just at that moment Isabel and Peter had arrived as they had finished their lessons for the day. Isabel, Peter, Jack and Victoria held hands, and the Wizard waved his wand, but the spell didn't seem to work.

'Perhaps we need more of us to come along and concentrate in order to make the spell work,' said the Wizard.

Peter ran through the woods and to Pixie Cottage to fetch Timon and Aster. They arrived back and together sang a song as part of the Wizard's spell. Once again it was the Blue Mist that appeared and encircled Jack and his dog. A few moments passed and sure enough Jack stepped out of the Mist and the children saw a wonderful thing that he had become an ordinary boy again. Dexter was just like any other dog and barked as if to say hello.

Everyone danced around in a circle in joy.

'Victoria,' said Jack pausing for a moment. 'Wouldn't you like to be as you were before instead of being a ghost?'

'Oh, don't worry about me,' said Victoria. 'I have a lot more work to do as a ghost, so I can help people this way.'

'Now,' said Victoria. 'I have spoken to Mrs. Allbright to see if she could look after you.'

'Oh that's wonderful,' said Jack. 'Both myself and Dexter can have our own home!'

Jack sat in a chair in a corner of the Wizard's cottage with Dexter by his side. Everyone smiled and Dexter barked as if to say hello.

'Yes Jack,' said Peter. 'Now you can join in our games with Timon and Aster.'

Later that evening, Isabel and Peter were in their bedroom. Aunt Emma was sitting in front of the fire with her embroidery. Twinkle the cat had curled up on the hearthrug. Just then Simpson the butler came in.

'Shall I make up the fire for tonight m'lady?' he said.

'No, Simpson, that will be all for this evening,' replied Aunt Emma. 'Can you ask Mrs. Jones to make hot chocolate for the children.'

Once the chocolate drinks were made, Aunt Emma brought them on a tray to Isabel and Peter. Victoria was talking to the children and vanished just as Aunt Emma came in.

'Oh my goodness children, you always seem to be out in the woods. Oh well. Enjoy your cocoa and don't forget to learn your poems ready for Mrs Spence's lesson tomorrow,' she said. 'Who were you talking to just now?'

'Errm,' said Peter trying to think of something clever to say. 'Errm, we were just talking to each other.'

'Oh well, never mind,' said Aunt Emma. As she left, she could hear the children giggling and smiled to herself.

Victoria re-appeared.

'Phew that was close,' she said.

'So tomorrow is Sunday. In the afternoon, let's meet Jack and his dog and we'll take him up to Greenthorpe Windmill,' suggested Peter.

Isabel and Peter took a basket of fruit with them and rode up to the Windmill on a pony and trap driven by Simpson. Jack and his dog were waiting for them at the end of the lane.

'Come back for us, Simpson, in an hour at this same spot,' said Peter.

'Yes, Master Peter,' said Simpson.

The children walked up the lane through the woods with Jack so he could meet with Mr. and Mrs Allbright at Greenthorpe Windmill.

'What if they don't like me?' said Jack looking sorrowful as his dog Dexter whimpered.

'She will. I'm sure and then they can take care of you now you're a boy,' said Isabel.   They all walked towards the Windmill passing a copse of trees.   Suddenly at that moment, the pixies Timon and Aster put their heads out from out of the bushes.

'Hi Jack!' said Aster. 'We came to wish you well in your new home.'   Timon and Aster hugged Jack and just then Victoria appeared as well.

'Go on Jack,' said Victoria. 'Welcome to your new home!'

'Oh my goodness!   Thank you all for saying hello,' said Jack looking wonderfully smart.

Just at the moment, the Wizard also stepped out of the trees.

'Ho. I wanted to pop in as well,' said the Wizard.

'Ha ha,' said Jack. 'Everyone is here.'

Isabel and Peter knocked on the door of the Windmill and left the basket of fruit on the doorstep and ran back to the trees out of sight. Mrs Allbright opened the door and wiped her hands on her apron.

'Hello Jack,' said Mrs. Allbright.

Jack was a little shy at first and looked back to the trees where he saw the children.

'Go on, Jack,' whispered Isabel from the trees.

There was a pause for a moment.

'Wizard,' asked Victoria by the trees. 'Can you cast one of your magic spells to create a time of happiness for Jack.?'

'Ha ha,' replied the Wizard. 'No magic is needed, Victoria. The real magic is that Jack I'm sure will find his happiness without my spells.'

'Hello Jack,' said Mr. Allbright who had brought his horse to the front of the house.

'There's a lovely meal waiting for you by the fire if you would like to come in?' said Mrs. Allbright.

Jack turned to the trees, and saw Isabel, Peter, Victoria and the Wizard.

'Go on, Jack, they like you,' said Victoria mouthing the words to him from the trees.

Jack turned to Mrs Allbright, there was a long pause and suddenly he smiled.

'Yes, Mrs Allbright, I would love to come in,' said Jack.

'Welcome to your new home, Jack,' said Mrs. Allbright with tears of joy.

Jack came forward and hugged Mr and Mrs Allbright and his dog Dexter jumped up and down with joy and barked. Mrs Allbright thanked Jack for the basket of fruit which she picked up. She turned around and noticed Victoria in the trees.

Victoria from a distance, mouthed the words, 'I can count on you.'

Mrs. Allbright replied brimming with happiness, 'Yes, you can count on me, Victoria.'

'Who are you talking to Martha,' said Mr. Allbright leading his horse back to the stable.

'Ha ha,' laughed Mrs. Allbright. 'Just myself John, just myself.'

Jack was happy to find a new home and Isabel, Peter, Victoria, the Wizard, Timon and Aster danced around together in the woods in a circle.

It was starting to get late, so Isabel and Peter ran down to the clearing where Simpson said he would meet the children in the pony and trap.

'Ha ha. Slow down you lot,' shouted Victoria in a half-joking manner. 'Ghosts can't run very fast you know!'

They all laughed. Victoria vanished in order to meet the children at Dackworth Manor. The pixies went back to Pixie Cottage whilst the Wizard vanished in a puff of smoke. Simpson the butler arrived in the clearing to take Isabel and Peter back home to Backworth manor in the pony and trap.

It had been a lovely day. Jack had found a new happy home with the Allbrights. He became good friends with Victoria and the others and together and they would meet for picnics in the woods, play games and visit the Wizard in his cottage.

-oOo-

Chapter 6

The Magic Tree

One evening in Summer, Isabel, Peter and Victoria stayed for tea once again with the Tingleberrys at Pixie Cottage. The sun shone through the trees and the stream could be heard babbling its way through the woods.

'Have you heard about the Magic Tree in the clearing in the woods just behind our cottage, Victoria?' asked Mrs. Tingleberry pouring the tea. Timon and Aster were playing draughts by the fire.

'Yes, we've seen it too,' said Aster.

'A magic tree?' said Peter. 'Shall we take a look, Victoria?'

Victoria smiled and took Isabel and Peter to see the Magic Tree in the woods nearby. Timon and Aster skipped along the lane with them.

'What's so special about this tree Victoria?' asked Isabel.

'Whenever the breeze blows,' replied Victoria, 'its leaves flutter and there is a musical sound that is like people singing in a choir. The Wizard told me that whoever hears the sound will decide to do a good deed and something wonderful happens.'

'That sounds lovely,' said Peter.

They all sat down by the tree. Timon brought out her flute and played a merry tune whilst Victoria sang to them. There was a lovely song that suddenly came from the tree in the background as its leaves fluttered. Just then the Wizard appeared in a puff of smoke.

'Oh my goodness,' said Isabel. 'Where did you come from, Mr. Wizard?'

'Ho,' said the Wizard. 'I heard Victoria singing. Yes, I have heard also that if someone does something wrong or they are unhappy, the singing of the tree works its magic and those who listen to its song are charmed into goodness and even become well again.'

'Yes. I have heard this too, Wizard. Come along, children, it's getting late, we must be getting back over the stream,' said Victoria.

Timon and Aster headed back to the Pixie Cottage and the Wizard vanished and Isabel and Peter returned through the path in the woods to

Backworth Manor. When they arrived back at the Manor, they could see that Aunt Emma had been reading the newspaper that the messenger boy had delivered and she seemed upset.

'What is it,' asked Isabel coming close and kneeling by the settee.

'Oh dear,' replied Aunt Emma. 'I have just read that a thief has broken into Applethorpe School and taken some of the food that we had brought for their Harvest Festival.

'Oh no!' gasped Peter.

Victoria had suddenly appeared on the landing behind the bannisters. *Perhaps it's another mystery that can be solved,* she thought. She was listening to see if she can help.

Aunt Emma rang for Simpson the butler.

'Ah. Simpson,' she said when he arrived. 'Can you take the pony and trap down to Applethorpe Police Station and ask Inspector Brown if he has any more information about a break-in at the local school.'

'Yes, m'lady,' replied Simpson.

Later in the day, after their lessons, unseen in the garden of the Manor, the children called for Victoria.

'Sorry to hear about the theft of the Harvest Festival food,' said Victoria when she appeared.

'Come with me, children. My friends, the wood squirrels may be able to help us.'

They shortly met with the squirrels in the woods near Backworth Manor. They told Victoria, that they had seen a man break into Applethorpe School and that he had hid in a shed at the edge of the woods. The wood squirrels guided Isabel and Peter and Victoria to the shed where the man was hiding. Victoria vanished and re-appeared inside the shed where she found a man with a sack who was sleeping. He seemed to be aware that Victoria was there and slowly opened his eyes.

'Aargh,' he gasped suddenly. 'It's a ghost!'

'My name is Victoria. You took the food,' she said. 'You're a thief! My friends the wood squirrels have told me!'

'Erm. Eh?' said the man. 'The squirrels? Gosh this surely is all a dream. My name is Edward. Look. I can see you are a ghost, but I wanted you to know that I didn't mean to take the food, Victoria. It's just that I was out of a job and my children needed some food, so I took some fruit and loaves, and scones.'

Just then, Isabel and Peter came into the shed. Victoria felt sad that the man's children had gone without food.

'Wait. Look, come with us, Edward,' said Victoria.

'Where are we going to?' he asked.

'It's a magic tree we want you to see,' said Isabel.

'Oh my goodness,' said Edward. 'First, it's a ghost, now it's talking squirrels, and now a magic tree! What's going on?'

'Ha ha,' said Peter. 'Don't worry, Mr. Edward, just come along and see. Come with us.'

As they walked, the squirrels ran around and one of them ran up and sat on Edward's shoulder.

'Ho,' said Edward regretting now he had taken the food and slept in the shed. 'This is all a dream surely.'

The closer that Edward came to the Magic Tree, the more he heard the sweetest melody of all which came from the tree itself as the leaves fluttered.

Victoria and the children danced around the tree with the squirrels.

'Children,' said Edward. 'The music reminds me of when I use to sing songs to my own children Jimmy and Anne. I feel charmed by this music and feel quite different.'

Suddenly, Edward put the sack down that he had with the fruit and food he'd taken.

'Victoria,' he said. 'I don't understand everything that is happening to me, but can you and the children take this sack and the food back to the school please. I am sorry I took it.'

Just at that moment, the loveliest melody that was ever heard came from the tree.

'I don't know what is happening to me,' said Edward. 'It's certainly a lovely song that I can hear. I want to go now to Applethorpe Police Station to confess what I've done and that I was the thief.'

'Look,' said Victoria. 'If you explain everything to Inspector Brown and the reasons for taking the food, I'm sure it will be all right.'

'Okay thanks,' said Edward. 'I'm on my way to the police station.'

After Edward had gone, the Wizard suddenly appeared in a puff of smoke wearing his pointed hat and holding his wand. Timon and Aster had also run to the tree when they heard the lovely song.

'The tree has sung its song and has really worked its magic!' said the Wizard.

The next day, Edward had an interview with Inspector Brown. Inspector Brown was puffing his pipe and a police constable was also in the room.

'So, your name is Edward Whitham?' asked the inspector.

'Yes,' replied Edward.

Suddenly, Victoria appeared in the room hiding behind a filing cabinet. When Edward saw her, he looked astonished, Victoria put her fingers to her lips indicating that Edward should keep quiet and say nothing.

Oh my goodness, thought Edward. *It's that ghost again!*

Just then Inspector Brown left the room. At that moment Victoria moved forward and blew all the papers over the place and quickly vanished.

Inspector Brown re-entered the room, and gasped when he saw all the papers he had written about the theft were now all over the place.

'Oh my goodness,' said the inspector. 'What have I done with your statement? Well, have you anything else that you would like to add Mr. Whitham?'

'Well,' said Edward with a sigh. 'It's like this. I met a ghost and then we went to a field and saw a magic tree that sang a song. Then two children and some squirrels danced around with the ghost and the squirrels scurried off, and I decided I would come to the police station. Erm. Do you believe me?'

The inspector paused for a moment.

'Aha ha!' Laughed the inspector. 'What a tale! Ho. You expect me to believe it?'

'Erm,' said Edward. 'Well, actually yes.'

The inspector laughed.

'Mr. Whitham,' he said. 'Just return all the food you took, and go home to your children. This time it's a caution, and please stay out of trouble.'

Yes,' said Edward smiling. 'I intend to stay out of trouble.'

Outside Applethorpe Police Station, Isabel and Peter were hiding behind the trees with Victoria. Edward saw them as he walked down the lane to his house.

'Hi everyone. This all seems like a dream, but I can't deny the magic of the tree has helped me. Has the sack of food been returned to the school? I need to go home now to make sure my children are okay,' said Edward.

'Yes. We've returned the food. Why don't you bring your children and wife as well to hear the Magic Tree?' asked Victoria.

'Ha ha,' said Edward.' I never thought I would be talking to a ghost. I'll certainly bring Jimmy, my young son to the singing tree. Although he can only walk with a crutch at the moment.'

'I'm sure the lovely song of the tree will cheer him up,' said Victoria.

The next day on Sunday morning, the children helped Aunt Emma tidy the rooms and assisted her with the housework as it was Simpson's day off. Mrs. Spence called in to say hello and help Mrs. Jones who was busy cooking something tasty for lunch later that day filling the house with a lovely aroma of freshly baked bread. Aunt Emma decided to have a nap by the fire and Twinkle the cat slept on her lap.

Isabel and Peter cycled to the Magic Tree, and they put their Penny Farthing bicycles by the trees nearby. Just then Edward had arrived by pony and trap, and was joined by his wife Elspeth, his daughter Anne and his son Jimmy. Edward's son Jimmy walked forward with his crutches towards the tree which immediately gave out a lovely song as its leaves fluttered.

'Jimmy,' said Isabel. 'Why don't you reach forward and touch the tree?'

'Go on Jimmy,' said Anne. 'This is your moment.'

Jimmy walked forward with his crutches towards the tree which immediately gave out a sweet song as its leaves fluttered and suddenly Jimmy laid his crutches on the ground and walked slowly towards the tree.

'Mummy, Mummy,' said Jimmy. 'I can walk again and I don't need my crutches.'

'It is a wonderful thing that has happened!' replied his mother.

Jimmy walked back to his mother, father and sister and hugged them.

'What a wonderful song from the Magic Tree!' said Peter.

Edward turned around and suddenly saw Victoria hiding in the trees nearby and waving.

You were right, Victoria, thought Edward to himself. Then he said aloud, 'The tree has worked it's magic and my son can walk again.'

'Who are you talking to?' asked Elspeth, holding Jimmy's hand.

Edward smiled.

'Just talking to myself, Elspeth. Things will be different now. Jimmy can walk again,' said Edward.

Jimmy skipped around with his sister Anne by the tree.

'Yes. Jimmy is well again,' said Elspeth. 'Thank you, Isabel and Peter.'

Isabel curtseyed and Peter bowed politely. Edward expressed his thanks to the children, and began walking back to the pony and trap with his wife, and Jimmy and Anne. Just at that moment Anne looked towards the nearby trees and saw some movement and heard giggling. There she saw Victoria and the two pixies, Timon and Aster. Anne ran to the trees, and she could see that Victoria was a ghost.

'Hi there,' said Anne. 'My name is Anne, what's yours?'

Victoria smiled. Anne could see through her to the trees behind her.

'Hi,' said Victoria. 'Please to meet you. I'm a ghost. You are not afraid of me, are you?'

'No. I'm not afraid,' replied Anne.

Just then Aster and Timon came forward from where they were hiding behind the trees and giggled.

'Hi,' said Anne skipping around a tree stump noticing their pointed ears and the hats they were wearing with a bell on the top.

'Hi Anne, my name is Timon and this is my brother Aster,' said Timon.

They told Anne that they were pixies. Anne was not afraid at all and said that she was glad that she had made new friends.

'I am so happy the magic tree helped Jimmy and now he can walk again,' said Anne. 'I can see that my mother and father are at the bottom of the slope waiting in the pony and trap, so I'll need to go now.'

They all went back to the singing tree in the middle of the clearing near the stream that led to Pixie Cottage. The squirrels came scurrying back and one of them climbed up on to Anne's shoulder and she laughed.

'Hello Mr. Squirrel!' said Anne who could hear the sounds he was making. Victoria came forward.

'The squirrel is saying hello to you and he is pleased to meet you,' said Victoria. 'But Anne, you mustn't tell anyone that you've seen me. It has to be a secret.'

'Yes, that's fine,' said Anne. 'Gosh, Victoria! You can even speak to squirrels!'

Victoria laughed.

'Thank you, Magic Tree,' said Victoria. 'It's been a lovely day.'

'Come along, Anne,' shouted Edward from the pony and trap at the bottom of the slope. 'We're waiting for you!'

Anne waved goodbye.

'I'm sure we'll meet again,' said Victoria. Just then, the Magic Tree began to sing again. Anne ran down the slope to the pony and trap joining her family. Timon and Aster said their goodbyes and returned to Pixie Cottage.

The children made their way along the path to Backworth Manor along with Victoria and the Magic Tree ceased its song.

Edward who had apologised for taking the food from the school, accepted a police caution from Inspector Brown. He didn't mention to anyone that he had met Victoria and Jimmy his son increased in health and no longer needed his crutches. Isabel and Peter became friends with Jimmy and Anne and they had further adventures together around the woods of Backworth Manor and by the stream.

One sunny evening, back at Backworth Manor, Isabel and Peter were learning their geography homework in their bedroom when Victoria appeared to them.

'Hi Victoria. Does the Magic Tree sing to everyone?' asked Peter.

Victoria sat down in the rocking chair in the corner. The children knelt down either side of her.

'The Magic Tree only sings to people who believe that they can be helped by its magic,' said Victoria. 'Maybe Jimmy and Mr. Edward somehow guessed that even before it began its song.'

The children closed their geography books as it was getting late. The children fell asleep snug in their beds. Victoria vanished and re-appeared behind the bannisters on the landing later that evening. She could see the roaring of the fire and hear the nightjars singing. Aunt Emma had fallen asleep by the armchair by the fire. Mrs. Jones had finished cleaning up in the scullery. Twinkle the cat then woke up and saw Victoria, meowed and jumped in front of the fire and yawned and sprawled out on the carpet.

'Yes,' whispered Victoria, so that Aunt Emma could not hear her. 'All is well. Everything is fine, Twinkle. Are you going to keep Isabel and Peter company this evening?'

Twinkle meowed and ran up the staircase and pushed open Isabel and Peter's bedroom door with its paw, and prowled around. She then jumped on to Isabel's bed, curled up in a ball and fell fast asleep. Victoria smiled. *Today had been a good day,* she thought. The fire burned

low in the hearth and evening had come. Then
Victoria vanished.

-oOo-

Chapter 7

The Musical Concert

One morning, in late summer, it had been raining and the sun was just starting to shine. The children had just finished their lesson with Mrs. Spence.

'You've done very well children in your studies, and you've completed your homework for your geography lesson,' said Mrs. Spence.

The children put their slates, crayons and pencils away, but Mrs. Spence their governess was unusually silent.

'Is there anything wrong?' asked Isabel.

'Well, I didn't like to mention it,' replied Mrs. Spence wiping away a tear, 'but I spoke to your Aunt Emma at lunchtime, and she seemed really upset.'

'I wonder what that could be about,' said Peter.

After their lesson, the children went into the sitting room and saw Aunt Emma crying whilst sitting in the armchair.

'Whatever is the matter?' asked Isabel, kneeling by the armchair. Just then Victoria appeared behind the curtains. She peeped through them, to see what was happening as she was worried about Aunt Emma and wanted to help.

'Oh dear,' said Aunt Emma. 'I don't know how I am going to manage to pay these huge bills for the coal, and the rent for the Manor and the grounds.'

'Is it a lot of money?' asked Peter.

'Yes, quite a bit, children,' sighed Aunt Emma, holding the bills in her hand. 'I'm really sorry, but I may need to sell Backworth Manor.'

Isabel and Peter looked very sad and gasped.

'Don't worry, children,' said Aunt Emma. 'I'll think of something. I'll ring for Simpson to bring me some tea and I'll have an afternoon nap.'

Thinking about these things, the children went for a walk through the stables and into the rose garden. Peter picked up Twinkle as she meowed and prowled around.

'Oh dear,' said Peter to Isabel. 'What are we going to do to help Aunt Emma?'

'I know,' said Isabel, 'let's call Victoria to help us. What do you think, Twinkle?'

The cat jumped down from Peter's arms and meowed as if to call Victoria.

Suddenly Victoria appeared as the children walked behind the rosebushes in the garden.

'Here I am, children!' said Victoria. 'Yes. Twinkle has just told me that Aunt Emma was upset that she was unable to pay her bills. I also heard everything when I was behind the curtains in the living room.'

They all stepped back into the edge of the woods so that they couldn't be seen from the Manor.

'Yes,' said Isabel who sobbed a little. 'Aunt Emma was upset and was crying in her chair. Oh Victoria, we can't lose Backworth Manor. We'll never see you again.'

Isabel shed some tears and Peter also looked very sad.

'Don't worry, children,' said Victoria. 'I'll never be far away from you and I'm sure we can think of a plan to raise money for Aunt Emma, so that she can keep Backworth Manor.'

'Oh, thanks, Victoria,' said Isabel, drying her tears and they hugged each other.

'Leave it to me and don't worry. I have already thought of a way to help,' said Victoria who smiled and vanished.

'Let's get back to the Manor for evening tea, Peter,' said Isabel.   'Then we have our geography homework to learn ready for lessons with Mrs Spence tomorrow.   Come on race you, Peter!

Isabel and Peter ran a race with each other back to the Manor entrance nearly knocking Simpson over when they arrived at the steps.

'Master Peter!' said Simpson. 'Erm, dinner is served.'

'Thank you, Simpson,' replied Peter.   'Er… sorry… in a bit of a hurry.'

Victoria appeared in Isabel and Peter's room later that night.   Isabel woke up and lit a candle. Twinkle then jumped off Isabel's bed and on to Peter's bed as if to say wake up.

'It's Victoria,' said Isabel. 'Come along, Peter, wake up.'

'Erm, what was that?' yawned Peter.

Victoria glided forward and smiled.

'Yes children, I have a plan and a way that we could possibly help your Aunt Emma and raise some money for her so that she can pay all her bills.'

The children suddenly were wide awake and excited waiting to hear her news.

'I have had a word with Mr. and Mrs. Tingleberry and Timon and Aster and all their pixie friends whilst visiting Pixie Cottage,' said Victoria. 'They are willing to put on a musical concert here at Backworth Manor to help raise funds for Aunt Emma. People in Applethorpe can then be invited to attend and maybe each person can be asked to make a donation for the concert. That could raise enough money to help Aunt Emma with her money difficulties.'

'Great,' said Peter. 'That sounds like a great idea. But when the guests see the pixies with their pointed ears, won't their secret in the woods be revealed and Pixie Cottage will be discovered?'

'I have thought of something,' said Victoria. 'The pixies can wear their woolly hats over their ears, and that way, no one will find out who they are, and their secret cottages in the woods will be safe.'

'I am sure they won't mind,' said Isabel.

'They are very keen to help,' said Victoria. 'Even the Wizard has agreed to support us.

The next day, the children and Victoria met at Pixie Cottage in the woods next to Backworth Manor. The Wizard had arrived so that he could cast one of his spells to help the pixie children to sing their lovely songs.

'There's a problem,' said Wizard. 'I can't use one of my spells until all the pixie children are willing to sing together. A young pixie called Trayton is over there and he is in a mood. He doesn't want to take part, and he's in the garden.'

'Let me see if I can help,' said Victoria

Victoria appeared to him in the garden.

'What's the matter, Trayton?' asked Victoria. 'Why are you sulking?'

'Hi Victoria. I've seen you before. You're Isabel and Peter's ghost friend. I know you're just trying to help, but my mother wanted me to do the washing up and I wanted to play with my toys instead,' replied Trayton looking down at the ground.

'But if you help us,' replied Victoria, 'then the Wizard can cast his spell, the children can sing and play wonderful music, and then the musical concert will be much better. We can then raise funds to help Aunt Emma.

Just then, a squirrel appeared in the garden, and started looking for nuts. Trayton gave the squirrel some nuts that he had in his pocket. Amazingly, the squirrel took the nuts and ran back to a nearby fence post and placed its tiny hand on Trayton's palm and then ran off again with the collected nuts. There was a long pause.

'Victoria!' said Trayton. 'The squirrel touched the palm of my hand!'

'Yes,' said Victoria. 'The squirrel said thank you. I understood what he said.'

Victoria began to glide back to the Tingleberry's cottage.

'Wait,' said Trayton. 'I'm coming back with you to help the Wizard. I've changed my mind. If I can do one good deed Victoria, I can do another. I'm sorry I was sulking.'

Inside Pixie Cottage, Isabel, Peter, Victoria and the Pixie children including Trayton held hands. The Wizard was able to cast his spell, and the choir sang some wonderful songs. Aster and Timon played their flutes and performed a lovely duet.

'That was wonderful,' said Isabel, clapping her hands.

'Yes, now at last, we can put on a concert at Backworth Manor and raise money to help Aunt Emma so that she can pay her bills and keep the Manor,' said Victoria. 'Anything that is left over we can donate to Hindlebury Children's Hospital in Applethorpe.'

Whilst the children were rehearsing in the garden of Pixie Cottage, Mr Tingleberry was ready with his piano accordion to play a melody for the pixie choir. Timon sung her lovely solo to everyone. Mrs. Tingleberry sang too and was accompanied by the accordion and the pixie choir sang their pieces.

'Here are the woolly hats you can wear,' said Mrs Tingleberry.' If you cover your ears, then the people from Applethorpe won't know our secret that we are pixies.'

Suddenly, Hector the Tingleberry's dog was startled and ran out into the nearby woods and started barking. Francesca, one of the pixies, ran out to find him.

'Come back, Hector,' shouted Francesca as she ran into the woods.

Victoria wanted to help, so she vanished and re-appeared outside the cottage.

'Francesca,' she shouted several times. 'Oh dear. It looks like she's gone missing. I need to find her as quickly as possible.'

As the children were on a break from their rehearsals, Victoria re-appeared back inside the cottage and asked for help to try and find Francesca.

'What shall we do?' asked Isabel.

Just then through the window, Victoria saw a crow circling above the garden and went outside. *I have an idea*, she thought.

'Crow, can you help us?' shouted Victoria as she glided into the garden. 'We need your help.'

'Hi Victoria,' said the crow, as he flapped his wings and settled down on the fence post.

Isabel and Peter joined Victoria in the garden.

'Gosh,' said Isabel. 'It's a crow who can speak.'

'Yes,' said Victoria. 'The Wizard gave him the power of speech. Crow, one of the pixies Francesca has run off to find her dog in the woods. We don't know where she is. Can you help us find her?'

'Oh Victoria,' said Crow.' Give me a break. I've been flapping my wings all day, and I need a nap.'

Peter came forward.

'Please, Mr. Crow,' said Peter. 'We need to find Francesca.'

The crow flapped his wings.

'Oh, all right, I'll help to find Francesca, but erm, will there be some lovely pieces of fresh bread set out for me in the garden when I get back?' said Crow.

Isabel and Peter said they would put out the bread for him on his return.

'Thanks, Crow,' said Victoria.

'Well, I'd better start to search then. Was it along the stream towards the woods?' asked Crow.

'Yes, she was running to find her dog Hector,' said Peter.

The Wizard told the choir inside the cottage, that they would have to halt the rehearsal as Crow flew off, circled round and headed towards the woods to try and find Francesca.

As he flew further, he could see a clearing below.

Ah thought Crow, *I'm sure that's Francesca. I'll fly down now.* As Crow flew down, he accidentally caught his leg on a twig, which bruised him and he spun around, but he could see Francesca holding Hector the dog.

'Francesca,' shouted the crow. 'Stay where you are and I'll guide you home to Pixie Cottage.'

'Hurry, Crow,' shouted Francesca. 'It's getting dark and I'm frightened.'

The crow landed, but limped a little, from his bruised leg and gasped.

'Crow, you're hurt!' said Francesca holding Hector and moving towards him.

'That's okay,' he replied. 'I'll guide you and Hector out of the woods this way. Just follow the flapping of my wings.'

As Francesca followed Crow, suddenly an angry stoat appeared and blocked their path. Crow flapped his wings to chase the stoat away who ran off. Although exhausted, Crow kept flapping his wings and guided Francesca and Hector the dog into another clearing where there was sunlight.

'Look,' said Francesca. 'There's the gate I ran through. Once we're through there, Pixie Cottage is along the lane. '

Hector barked as if in agreement, and Francesca and Hector were led by Crow through the gate and towards Pixie Cottage. Isabel and Peter and the children saw them and ran out of the cottage.

Victoria appeared outside to greet them.

'Thanks, Crow,' said Victoria. 'I knew you could find Francesca and Hector. But oh dear, I can see you're hurt!'

Crow limped a little and felt exhausted.

'It's okay,' he said. 'I guess I should have watched where I was going. There was this stoat who was in a bad mood and wouldn't move out the way in the woods and took a swipe at my feathers. Gee-whizz.'

'Yes,' said Francesca. 'Crow was very brave.'

'Hey Crow,' said Isabel. 'Sit on this tray, and we'll carry you to the cottage. We have some

delicious bread pieces for you and a cool saucer of water waiting for you.'

'Thanks, you guys,' replied Crow. 'I guess it was long overdue for me to help someone. Hey everyone. Let's get your choir going. It sounded great.'

Once they were all inside Pixie Cottage, Crow felt much better, Francesca was with Hector the dog, and the pixie choir sang along with Isabel and Peter their lovely songs and they were all ready for the concert at Backworth Manor.

Sure enough, when Sunday afternoon came along, the pixie children had put leaflets around in Applethorpe advertising their musical concert at 7 p.m. that very evening at Backworth Manor. Admission was free, but donations were welcome.

Isabel and Peter had kept the concert a secret from Aunt Emma but spoke with Simpson, Mrs. Jones and Mrs Spence about their plans. Just as all the guests from Applethorpe started to arrive at the Manor steps, Isabel and Peter guided them into the living room. Inspector Brown was among the guests and he helped to get everyone seated. The time came for Isabel and Peter to find Aunt Emma who was in her office. They knocked on the door. Aunt Emma opened it and wondered what was going on.

'Aunt Emma,' said Isabel crossing her fingers behind her back. 'Some of our friends have arrived to provide a musical concert for you.'

'A concert for me?' gasped Aunt Emma as Isabel and Peter took her into the living room.

Isabel, Peter and the pixies along with Mr and Mrs. Tingleberry were all assembled in the living room to present their musical performance and Simpson the butler had helped the choir to set up.

As soon as Aunt Emma entered the living room, there was a round of applause from the smiling guests.

'Simpson,' said Aunt Emma. 'Why did you not tell me all these people were coming?'

'Well, m'lady,' replied Simpson not really knowing what to say.

'Aunt Emma,' said Isabel, 'the children are all waiting to present their music and song.'

Aunt Emma smiled and she sat in an armchair at the front of the living room which was full of residents from Applethorpe dressed in their Sunday best.

'Simpson,' she said smiling. 'Please ask the children to sing.'

The pixie children's choir stood up at the front and along with Isabel and Peter sang their musical pieces accompanied by Mr Tingleberry on the piano accordion. Timon sang a beautiful solo and both Timon and Aster played their flutes. Mrs Tingleberry conducted the pixie choir and they sang beautifully.

After the concert, all the people from Applethorpe who attended applauded. Isabel and Peter came forward with an earthenware pot that they had borrowed from the scullery filled with coins and bank-notes that all the people had donated.

'Aunt Emma,' said Peter. 'This is for Backworth Manor.'

'Yes,' said Isabel. 'Now you can keep Backworth Manor for ever!'

The whole of the audience applauded and Mrs. Jones wiped away a tear from her eye.

'But children,' said Aunt Emma standing up, 'I am overjoyed that you have helped me and there is more than enough money here to pay all the bills, but I couldn't possibly accept this gift.'

Just then Inspector Brown stepped forward.

'Ma'am,' said Inspector Brown. 'Speaking on behalf of all these residents of Applethorpe. Please accept these donations. This has been a lovely evening of music and song. Master Peter and Miss Isabel and the rest of these young people have brought us some happy moments over these last few weeks.'

There was a great cheer and warm applause. Victoria was just to the side of a cabinet at the top of the stairs. *I don't want everyone to see me*, she thought. *This has been so wonderful for the children and Aunt Emma!*

'I am so grateful for this gift everyone, children and people of Applethorpe,' said Aunt Emma. 'May Backworth Manor always be a place of peace and spreading cheer and happiness for Applethorpe. This gift has been a lovely gesture. Thank you everyone!'

Aunt Emma hugged Isabel and Peter, and Victoria at the top of the bannisters clapped her hands with glee.

'But we have no refreshments for our guests,' said Aunt Emma.

Just then Mrs. Jones the cook helped by Mrs. Spence brought out a trolley of lovely cakes, jellies and ice cream and sandwiches.

'Oh m'lady,' said Mrs. Jones. 'I'm really sorry, but we were in, on the secret as well!'

Aunt Emma laughed and the children's choir sang again conducted by Mrs. Tingleberry. Then the refreshments were served to everyone. Some of the guests sat on chairs and the children sat on the carpet. It had been a lovely concert.

Just then where Victoria stood behind the bannisters, Crow flew in through the window and perched beside her.

'Hi Crow,' said Victoria. 'I thought you were taking a nap?'

'Hi Victoria,' said the crow flapping his wings. 'I guess I just couldn't miss the party. Ha ha.'

At that moment some smaller crows flew in.

'Erm,' said Crow. 'Meet Mrs. Crow and the family!'

Victoria laughed.

'Welcome everyone!' replied Victoria.

Mrs. Jones assisted by Simpson and Mrs. Spence had created a wonderful tea with jelly and ice cream, which they served to all the children and the guests and made certain no-one was left out. There was much laughter and everyone was happy. Even Inspector Brown and his constables were sitting down having tea.

Victoria disappeared from behind the bannisters and re-appeared behind the curtains. Isabel and Peter came over to the curtain and whispered to Victoria that they had seen Jack and his dog Dexter whom she had helped earlier. Jack saw Victoria, who waved back.

'Jack,' said Victoria. 'You came.'

'Yes,' replied Jack. 'I couldn't miss this concert. I know you're a ghost, but I still wanted to shake your hand.'

'That's okay,' laughed Victoria. 'This has been a lovely day.'

At that moment, Isabel, Peter and Victoria looked through the window and saw two children dressed in rags looking very sad as they stood by the gates of the Manor. One of the girls was holding her doll.

'They must have heard the music and laughter and made their way up from Applethorpe,' said Victoria.

'Victoria!' whispered Isabel. 'The children and the person who I think is her mother look quite ill and hungry.'

'Yes, I've seen them. Jack, why not invite them in to share in this lovely food and time of laughter,' replied Victoria.

Jack went outside into the garden and invited the children and their mother into the living room. Peter brought a tray across to them of sandwiches, cake and ice cream.

'Oh thank you!' said the mother. The children smiled and together with their mother they came into the Manor for something to eat and sat down.

'Mummy, Mummy, this jelly and ice cream is lovely,' said one of the children. 'Come along, Mummy, you can have some too.'

Just then Aunt Emma came over and Victoria hid behind the curtain. Isabel wondered what Aunt Emma would say as there was a pause when she saw the children.

'Mrs. Jones,' smiled Aunt Emma. 'Please bring over some more hot tea for our guests. Most welcome.'

The children and their mother were so happy. The pixie choir sang once more and Aunt Emma made a speech saying thank you to everyone. Backworth Manor was safe again and it had been a wonderful evening for everyone with beautiful music, food and friendship.

When it was time to go home, Mr. and Mrs Tingleberry made certain all the pixie children were gathered together safely and Jack and his dog helped them. Simpson the butler used the pony and trap to take some of the children home. Inspector Brown and his constables used their horse and carriage to take some of the parents back to Applethorpe as well. Mrs. Jones the cook, helped by Mrs. Spence the governess cleared up the living room after the musical concert and washed the dishes and tidied up.

Aunt Emma locked the money raised in a safe place and returned to her armchair by the fire. Isabel and Peter sat aside her chair. Mrs Jones brought a cup of cocoa to Aunt Emma, and Simpson made sure that the Manor was secure for the night.

'Isabel and Peter,' said Aunt Emma. 'Your parents would be so proud of you.'

'Now you can keep Backworth Manor, Aunt Emma,' said Isabel.

'Thank you, children. You all sang so well, and the choir also sang beautifully,' said Aunt Emma.

Aunt Emma retired for the evening and slept well knowing that Backworth Manor was safe. Isabel and Peter then went back up to their rooms.

'You sing louder than me Isabel,' said Peter.

'Ha ha. We make a good duet then,' replied Isabel. 'Yes. It was a lovely concert.'

Later. Isabel and Peter were asleep when suddenly there was a bolt of lightning and the sound of thunder and then the bedroom windows flew open. The children sat up in their beds.

'Victoria, Victoria, where are you?' shouted Isabel.

Victoria suddenly appeared at the base of the bed.

'Here I am, children!' said Victoria smiling.

'Oh Victoria,' said Peter rubbing his eyes and lighting a candle. 'We had a bad dream.'

'Don't be afraid, children, and don't worry,' said Victoria.

Twinkle jumped down from Isabel's bed and meowed.

'Yes, Twinkle,' said Victoria. 'Twinkle says, don't be afraid, it's only a storm.'

Peter quickly got out of bed and closed the windows and drew the curtains and got back into bed again.

'Please sing us a song tonight,' asked Isabel.

'Ha ha, of course,' said Victoria who found a way of sitting in the rocking chair in the bedroom. She sung her lovely song to Isabel and Peter. She stepped forward and Isabel and Peter and hugged her.

'Friends always,' said Victoria.

'Friends always,' replied Isabel and Peter.

'Thanks for arranging the musical concert. We love you, Victoria,' said Isabel.

'I love you too,' replied Victoria.

The children fell fast asleep and then Victoria vanished. A few moments later she re-appeared in the room, sat in the chair and watched over Isabel and Peter until the storm had passed. *All is well*, thought Victoria. *It had been a lovely day and Backworth Manor was safe.* She blew out the candle and disappeared. Tomorrow would be another day of adventures.

Ingram Content Group UK Ltd.
Milton Keynes UK
UKHW040613250623
423977UK00003B/15

9 781803 698762